FIRST LOOK AT

CARS

For a free color catalog describing Gareth Stevens' list of high-quality children's books, call 1-800-341-3569 (USA) or 1-800-461-9120 (Canada).

Library of Congress Cataloging-in-Publication Data

Butler, Daphne, 1945-
   [Cars]
   First look at cars / Daphne Butler.
      p. cm. -- (First look)
   Previously published as: Cars. c1990.
   Includes bibliographical references and index.
   Summary: A simple introduction to the history and uses of cars and
their effect on our world.
   ISBN 0-8368-0503-8
   1. Automobiles--Juvenile literature. [1. Automobiles.] I. Title.
   II. Series: Butler, Daphne, 1945- First look.
   TL147.B867   1991
   629.222--dc20   90-10265

North American edition first published in 1991 by

Gareth Stevens Children's Books
1555 North RiverCenter Drive, Suite 201
Milwaukee, Wisconsin 53212, USA

U.S. edition copyright © 1991 by Gareth Stevens, Inc.   First published as *Cars* in Great
Britain, copyright © 1990, by Simon & Schuster Young Books. Additional end matter
copyright © 1991 by Gareth Stevens, Inc.

Photograph credits: Mothercare, 23; Topham, 8, 9, 11; ZEFA, all others

Series editor: Rita Reitci
Design: M&M Design Partnership
Cover design: Laurie Shock

Printed in the United States of America

2 3 4 5 6 7 8 9 97 96 95 94 93 92 91

FIRST LOOK AT

CARS

DAPHNE BUTLER

Gareth Stevens Children's Books
MILWAUKEE

CONTENTS

DREAM CARS

Do you have a dream car? Is there one you would really like to have a ride in?

There are hundreds of different cars. Some are new, some old. Some are fast, some slow. Do you have a favorite?

OVER A HUNDRED YEARS AGO

Before there were cars, people walked, rode on horseback, or traveled by coach or carriage.

These early cars look more like carriages than the cars we know today. How fast do you think they could travel?

EN 1903. — LE PASSAGE D'UNE AUTOMOBILE DANS UN PETIT VILLAGE D'ANGLETERRE

Composition de L. THACKERAY. (Musée de la Voiture et du Tourisme, à Compiègne.)

A FEW YEARS LATER

At the beginning of the twentieth century, cars were still a rare sight. People used to stand and stare whenever a car passed by.

Most people couldn't afford cars. They were expensive and often broke down.

RULES OF THE ROAD

People thought the new cars were dangerous,
so they made rules about how fast they could go.

In Britain people decided cars should ride on the
left side of the road. But in most other countries,
cars ride on the right.

13

LICENSE PLATES

With so many cars on the roads, people had to figure out a way to identify them. That's why cars have license plates.

Can you guess where these license plates come from?

15

16

SUPERMARKET

GOING PLACES

Cars are very popular for many reasons. In a car you can go where you like, whenever you like.

A car can carry things and pull trailers.

What other uses can you think of?

18

RACING CARS

From the time cars were first built, people liked to race them.

Sometimes races are held on racetracks with specially built cars.

What other kinds of races can you think of?

REPAIRING CARS

Have you ever been in a car when it had a flat tire?

Flat tires are easy to fix. But sometimes cars break down and won't start again. They need to go to the garage to be repaired.

SAFETY AND CARS

Cars can travel very fast. If they hit something, they can cause a lot of damage.

People can be badly hurt or even killed in a car crash. Make sure you wear your seat belt. It can save your life.

23

BUILDING NEW CARS

The first cars were built by hand in a workshop. It took months to finish just one car.

Today people use computers to help design and test new cars. Workers operate robots that build cars on a production line.

Thousands of cars can be built in a few days.

BUILDING NEW ROADS

The more cars people own, the more roads we need. New roads are being built all the time. Highways sprawl across the countryside.

Often people living in the country don't want new highways. Why do you think this is so?

TRAFFIC JAMS

More and more cars use the new roads. They often get into traffic jams. Have you ever been in a traffic jam? Can you remember how you felt?

We will always need cars. But how do we keep them from creating traffic jams?

29

More Books about Cars and Driving

Auto Mechanic. Imershein (Julian Messner)
Automobiles. Wilkinson (Childrens Press)
The Big Book of Real Race Cars and Race Car Driving. Slater
    (Putnam Publishing Group)
Cars. Langley (Franklin Watts)
Cars and Trucks. Thompson (Gareth Stevens)
Custom Cars. Barrett (Franklin Watts)
Fill It Up! Gibbons (Harper & Row Junior Books)
I Can Be a Race Car Driver. Wilkinson (Childrens Press)
Monster Trucks and Other Giant Machines on Wheels. Bushey (Carolrhoda)
Racing Cars. Petty (Franklin Watts)
See How It Works: Cars. Potter (Macmillan)
The Service Station. Dupasquier (Putnam Publishing Group)
Truck Driver. Stamper (Troll)
When I Ride in a Car. Chlad (Childrens Press)

Glossary

Computer: A machine with electronic parts that can help people quickly find the answer to a problem. The basic way of solving problems is built into the machine. Ways of solving particular kinds of problems can also be put into the computer. These particular ways are called programs.

Highway: A main road. Highways are usually wider than other roads. Cars can often travel faster on highways.

License plate: A metal plate with numbers and often letters that is fastened to the front or back of a car. Every license plate is different and is used to identify the car to which it is attached.

Production line: A method of making a car in a factory. The car moves along on a belt or track in front of the workers. Each worker does just one job on the car being built. Many factories use robots in place of human workers. Factories that make other kinds of things also use production lines.

Racing car: A car that is specially built for racing. It can go much faster than other cars. There are many kinds of racing cars, and they may drive only on racetracks or routes laid out for them.

Robot: A machine that can carry out a task that a skilled human used to do. The machine is controlled by a computer. The computer's program tells the machine exactly what to do.

Rules of the road: A set of rules that every person must obey when driving a car. Rules of the road tell drivers what they may and may not do while driving. By helping drivers know what to expect from other drivers, these rules make driving a car much safer and far more pleasant for all.

Index

A number that is in **boldface** type means that the page has a picture of the subject on it.

firnagd